A Quiet Place

A collection of poems about finding peace
and quiet in a crazy world

Lily Sticha

BookLeaf
Publishing

India | USA | UK

Dedication

This book is dedicated to anyone struggling with anxiety, depression, panic attacks, suicidal thoughts, or anyone struggling with their mental health.
 You are valid, you are worth it, you are loved and you *will* get through this.
Stay alive for me.

Preface

My goal for this book is for anybody who doesn't know me, to be able to get to know me through this book. This is not a biography but instead it is snippets of writing about the things I find most important to me, starting with some of my favorite poems that I wrote during my creative writing class, including my favorite "A quiet place"
 Some of these poems cover heavy topics around mental health, so please take caution if you are easily triggered, similarly some of them are about certain people in my life, and if you are one of those people you probably know who you are. but permission has been asked and names have been censored or removed to ensure privacy. This book is a little all over the place, but so am I.

Acknowledgements

I want to thank my creative writing teacher, who ~~made me~~ encouraged me to write, even when I didn't feel like it and for giving me lots of ideas to start this book off of, my Dad for making me laugh, and for always helping me problem solve, when it comes to life, and computers. And finally my mom, for loving me, and always being there for me especially when you were struggling yourself, you are and will always be my rock. I love you so much.

1. A Quiet Place

My head turns, heartbeat rising, anger builds inside of
me,
fist are clenched, mind is screaming, looking for a way to
escape.
There is no way out. This is MY room.
I need to find
My quiet place.

I panic, and tears begin to fall.
Thoughts run through my brain.
Angry, violent thoughts.
My mind tell me I'm a horrible person because
My world is turned upside down
All because of a sound.
I am still looking for
my quiet place.

I slam the door, run down the hall
Crying, screaming, choking.
It is the middle of the night and the world is sleeping
yet I am wide awake,
thinking I never want to go back there again.
But it is my room, I should feel safe there.
But I do not.

I look out at the window, at the stars and the street lights
Tears still streaming down my face
And I feel relief because I have found

My quiet place.

2. Palestine

If you look around, you can see smiling faces.
But this is not a happy event
Far from it.
The faces are simply the ones of those who are standing
proud during chaos, knowing
That they are doing the right thing.
People pushed, shoved being pushed to the ground, their
voices like daggers,
Crying out for their families.

It started with the "evictions"
a peaceful neighborhood, full of families, happy children.
Plucked from their homes without warning
Some ordered to destroy them with their own hands,
Never to be seen again.
Not for new people to move in
But for a theme park.

Next came the attacks on our mosque and their
worshippers.
Bombs set off inside, rubble scattered on the floor
Occupation cutting off worshippers from lifesaving
medical aid.
In the distance settlers can be heard cheering as a nearby

tree is set ablaze.
I know that our mosque cries for her people.
She may not be able to talk
But I know that she has a voice,
The voice that speaks through the people inside.

Next, came the war.

What you have heard is true,
The Resistance warned that if the settlers were to raid Al
Aqsa that they would attack.
And so they did.
Sirens can be heard from the other side.
More than 4,000 rockets seen soaring through the air
over the apartheid wall.
Most were intercepted.
Some reached their targets,
Others fell short, killing their own people
But as they kept their promise, so did their enemies.

 The occupation responded with full force.
Phosphorus bombs, airstrikes, showing no mercy
Whether you were a civilian, a child, or a designated
"terrorist"
Homes, hospitals, schools, news outlets, reduced to
rubble
Bombs like a blazing wall of fire and dust,

Sounds that damage the ears.
And sights that pierce the heart.
One can drive through the streets of the city and see
nothing but rubble for miles.

Finally, after 11 brutal days of fighting and hundreds of
lives lost, came the ceasefire.
It was a glorious day for everyone,
people everywhere can be heard cheering, crying,
hugging their families.
It was a rightful cause for celebration.
But I would like to point out that the streets of Gaza are
still ridden with rubble,
Those hundreds of lives, already lost.
The damage has already been done, and none of it can
ever go back to the way it was.

They say that Hamas were the first ones to attack.
I would argue that it was the ethnic cleansing of people
from their homes that started this war in the first place.
If that hadn't happened, this whole mess would've been
avoided. I do not condone violence in any way. But to
understand the situation, let's look at the history. This is
not the first time a city has faced this same type of fate.
Sheikh
Jarrah,   Silwan,   Jenin,   Al
Quds

Al Khalil,   Yaffa
Gaza
Syria
Iraq
Yemen
Kashmir

Ukraine

Afghanistan

East Turkestan

Somalia

Armenia

Kurdistan

Assyria

Turtle Island

....

Palestine.

3. Be the One You Love

"Be the one you love" it reads.
Words that I hold close to my heart
And that I hope will carry me through some of hardest
times.
"They're satanic"
"They look like girls"
"they're too emo and encourage self harm" people say
But how can they be when with words like this,
When their music has saved so many lives and helped so
many people?

Then tears begin to fall.
I feel like a failure,
Like nothing I ever do is good enough,
I've already failed 5 classes
and I wasn't about the fail another one.
This is one of first times I have felt this way,
Am I even smart enough for a physics major?
Went from "Gifted" in high school
 to struggling to pass my classes
Maybe I'm not cut out for it
Maybe I should give up of my dreams and passions

Then I remember the words strung around my neck,

I roll the tag around in my hand, clutch it tightly
And repeat the words in my head,
I was not a quitter,
I didn't quit last year when I told myself that I should
And I'm not going to now.

4. My Brain

My beloved asshole brain,
stops working sometimes.
Hilarious and awful,
not knowing down versus up.
Just a cup of dirty water,
use may vary.
No way to get started.

"I'll get to it later"

5. fisics

"Physics is physics"
my professor said. I wish
It was that easy.

6. Student Struggles

I have no idea what's going on
*Tears
my head exploded
Wait, what?
I don't know what I'm even doing
*Banging my head against a wall
*internal screaming
uuggghhhh
I just wanna go home
I need a nap
My brain hurts

7. Signs of Spring

Trees
And
Sunshine
Signs of spring
New life sprouting up
From the dead and cold of winter
Morning sun, evening walks, star shining upon the earth.

8. Path of Life

They say that the shortest distance between two points is
a straight line.
But that doesn't consider if it is raining or snowing,
if there are any potholes,
or if there is ice,
or wind blowing in your face,
or the fact that on a globe, the shortest distance between
two cities is a curve,
because of the curvature of the earth.

The arrow of time is a straight line that keeps marching
forward,
but sometimes your life seems like a twisty-turny path
through the forest.
Sometimes you go from having mental breakdowns from
losing your mind over noises one year,
to being successful in school, and getting your life back
together the next,
Sometimes you feel as lost as my mom trying to find her
way back home.
Sometimes that same disease that makes you cry because
your mother forgot where she lives
is the same one that makes you laugh because she leaves
the house without shoes.

People say obstacles in your path are meant to make you
stronger,
But some obstacles are nothing but nuisance,
other ones leave scars,
giant ones that take years to heal even after the damage
has already been done.
Other times, you wonder for far too long in one direction
and spend ages trying to get yourself back on track,
and by then you've already wasted your time

I spent ages wishing that my memories of last year
would go away
and even now I am still recovering
"If only I had just done that one thing differently, my life
would be so much better"
I wondered if I was a bad person.
I wondered why this once gentle person all the sudden
became filled with anger and hatred.
Other memories, while traumatic,
are very much a part of me,
and I believe were meant to happen for a specific reason.
I once thought that I knew exactly what was to come,
but instead I got lost and am only now starting to find
my way back.

While on this winding road,

you start to realize that the more you wander, wondering
where you are or where you're going,
the more you start to notice things you didn't before,
such as the flowers on the forest floor,
the sound of birds in the morning,
the way the sun shines through the canopy.

You learn to enjoy the simple pleasures,
to slow down to stop and smell the roses.
And most importantly, you learn that the most important
part of life,
is not the destination,
but the journey.

9. Cancer

Her hair coming out in clumps
patches of bare skin on her head
her nails peeled back at the edges
skin blistering and turning red.
Her stomach aches and her side hurts

she got flowers
candy,
cards,
meals made for her.
Everyone stopped to ask how she was doing,

I love my mom more than anything, but sometimes,
I couldn't help but wonder
Where were *my* flowers?

10. I Knew Love I

I thought I knew love until I met
him
Tiny little baby
could almost fit in the palm of his dad's hands.
I remember the day we were all standing on the stairs to
our rooms
everyone started cheering
I had no idea what was going on.
Until it hit me.

during quarantine everybody had to wait to see him
we were all waiting to get our hands on the baby.
his best friend was the dog
his first word was taco
I hear his screams as he begs for me to chase him around
the house
I remember the way he cares for his little siblings
"It's a choking hazard" he says

And I remember when he was signed up for preschool
"Are you going to school?" his parents asked
"Yes, just like Lily"

11. I Knew Love II

I thought I knew love until I met
them
Two tiny little babies
their sleeves covering their tiny hands
"coming soon!"
"me too"
the shirts on their announcement read

Dad spikes the boys hair into a mohawk
and puts a tiny little bow in the girl's like the cutest little
present.
"Did you know I'm a twin too? You're cuter though"

I love the way she dances every time there is music
or her tiny little giggles when you're playing with her
I love the way he always clings on his mom,
or the way he says hi to everyone passing by

I love the way they steal each other's pacis
and the way they throw their food across the room
because with children, even the annoying things become
adorable
that's how you know
you love them.

12. Sensitive

They say it is both a blessing and a curse to feel
everything so very deeply.

Sometimes it is a curse,
Because you find yourself crying for hours on end, over
something small,
sometimes so hard that you feel physically sick.
Every single harsh word, criticism, mean joke,
cuts so very deeply.
you find yourself wondering if there is something wrong
with you,
or why you can't stand up for yourself
instead of spiraling into a pit of self hatred.

Other times, it is a blessing
you feel love, passion, excitement much more intensely
you love like no other.
like a flame the engulfs your body,
filling you with comforting warmth,
the passion is what keeps you going when it's hard to go
on
you feel empathy for others,
because you relate to them,
like "I know how hard it is, because I've been there and I

know what it's like"

I think it's natural,
a part of being human
called the "fitra" in Arabic, meaning the innate tendency
to goodness.
As soon as a baby is born, they know nothing but to cry.
but yet it is the world that tells us to "toughen" up.
it is such a uniquely human thing
to feel.
to sense
to be in tune with the world around us.

I think that the world would be a better place
if we all followed our natural tendencies
and felt everything

a little more deeply.

13. Ode to my Bed

Like a warm embrace, it is the only thing I want.
an endless loop of "I just want to go to bed"

A place where all of my problems seem to melt away
just one touch of the soft blanket
and I instantly forget everything that ever bothered me

It is there for me when no one else is
like my best friend
"come rest you weary head" it beckons
"I know you are tired, let me take all your worries away"

14. The Universe

The Universe
never ceases to amaze me
so many big questions that we have yet to answer

how did the universe begin?
how will it end?
are we alone?
what happens if you fall into a black hole?
Are we one of many universes?
Like a grain of sand on a larger beach?

When you look up at the stars, you are looking back in
time.
because the light takes time to reach you
We are made from the elements that were formed from a
supernova of a dying star

Without space, I might not be here.
Not just because we were made of stardust,
but because it was my passion that kept me going

when I no longer wanted to live.

15. Dear little me

Follow your passions
Reach for the stars,
Trust in God.

life will get hard,
it will punch you, kick you spit at you,
but you will come back
stronger,
and you will wonder why you ever worried.

Remember everyone that came before you
who taught you, raised you, inspired you.
Imagine if they saw you now,
They would be so proud,
but more importantly
so am I.

16. Angels on Earth

Some people say that dogs are angels on earth.
that we do not deserve them
they comfort us when we are are sad
are always in-tune with our emotions
are our loyal companions.
want nothing but to please us and make us happy.
I guess that is why they call them "man's" best friend.
Some dogs can sniff out cancer,
some are service dogs,
other ones save lives.
others protect people from dangerous predators.

Mine steals socks.

17. Introvert

keep your head down
don't make eye contact
look ahead
don't look up
check your phone,
if they say hi, ignore them
if they smile at you ignore them
walk around them

Oh shoot- someone's coming, gotta go-

18. Love you like I do

You told me you hate yourself.
you told me you wanted to die.
You told you weren't good enough for me,
and that I deserved better

I do not put you on a pedestal,
and I hope you don't either,
rather, I see all of you, flaws and all.
you're ripped at every edge
but you're a masterpiece.*

and from the bottom of my heart I hope you are happy,
I hope she gives you the love that you deserve
that she helps you shine the light that you're hiding

because if you don't love yourself,
I will.

*from Halsey's "Colors".

19. My Voice

Through my music,
I am given a voice.

Through my songs
and the air from my lungs
and through the vibration of the strings
over a hollow wooden body:
I can make art,
a poem
a melody

For the quiet kid,
who sits in the back of the room,
who sometimes has trouble thinking of what to say,
who would rather be alone than in a room full of people,

music is what allows me to speak.
and with it,
I will never lower my voice.

20. Child of Two Worlds

I watched as people stare at my parents
I kept waiting for my life to flash before my eyes
to remember what happened in my first year of life.
My brain didn't remember but my heart did.
I heard my foster mother run into the orphanage
meeting room.
She was a total stranger to me, yet I felt like I had known
her my whole life.
I remember how she used to love me, care for me,
nurture me, and raise me.

I know nothing about my birth parents
It's not that this information is hidden or somehow
protected, it's because
It simply isn't there.
I was born and hours later I was found in a box
outside of an orphanage.
There was no report of my birth or who my parents
were.

This day in Xiaogan was one of the best days of my life.
I didn't get to meet my birth parents,
but I got to meet the people who cared for me after my
birth.

To the Chinese, I'm too "westernized," not disciplined
enough, too popular,
To the Americans, I'm seen as quiet, super smart, and
somebody who never gets in trouble.

They say that you're supposed to be able to find where
you belong.
The more I know who I am,
the more I realize I don't belong,
and I don't want to.
I am a child of two worlds.
 too Chinese for the Americans,
too American for the Chinese.

When people see me they forget that I've been playing
the cello for 17 years or that I love to write, or that I
have a passion for math and science and love astronomy
and want to continue studying it

I'm Chinese American but I'm also a person with big
dreams,
a big personality,
and a bright future ahead of me.

21. Tainted by Tragedy

October 7th
I was at a concert,
it was supposed to be one of the best days of my life

I used to say that everything reminds me of Black Veil
Brides,
their words, their riffs, their message
but now I know, that everything goes back to Palestine.
I can no longer think about them without thinking about
those children.
Every single lyric of every single song, reminds me of
them.

As a stare at my tshirt,
with the date printed clearly on it,
I wanted to destroy it, burn it,
throw it in the trash.

It was supposed to be a happy day,
but for so many, it was the worst,
and for so many others, it was their last.
How can I celebrate
when there are people dying,
children crying,

their limbs blown off by bombs.
How can I celebrate, the start of a such a horrible
tragedy
that had no ending in sight.
How can I celebrate a day that from now on will only be
remembered
as a day
tainted by tragedy

www.ingramcontent.com/pod-product-compliance
Lightning Source LLC
Chambersburg PA
CBHW071235140726
47996CB00007B/2619